I0531242

THE NARROW CHOICE

Christian Wisdom for Decisions You Won't Regret

by

James B. Fannin

Reviewed by John W. Lovitt, Ph.D., Ed.D., LPC

Published by JBF Ventures LLC

jbfventuresllc.com | jamesbfannin.com

James B. Fannin

Copyright

Copyright © 2025 James B. Fannin

All rights reserved.

All Scripture quotations are taken from the *New American Standard Bible* (NASB), © The Lockman Foundation. Used by permission. All rights reserved.

Reviewed by John W. Lovitt, Ph.D., Ed.D., LPC, for accuracy in interpreting and applying psychological and mental-health principles.

Cover design by James B. Fannin (AI-assisted)

Published by JBF Ventures LLC

Contact: jfannin627@outlook.com

ISBN: 979-8-9987271-2-2 (Print)
ISBN : 979-8-9987271-3-9 (eBook)

Disclaimer: This book is intended to provide biblical and psychological insights for personal growth and decision-making. It is not a substitute for professional counseling or therapy. Readers are encouraged to seek licensed professional guidance when needed.

2

For my wife –

Whose patient, prayerful heart has shaped my understanding of godly decision-making.

Through her steady example, I learned that wisdom is found not merely in knowledge, but in the grace to wait upon the Lord. This book is a tribute to her unwavering desire that we unite facts, faith, and feeling into the balanced discernment that reflects God's own heart.

"The wisdom from above is first pure, then peaceable, gentle, reasonable, full of mercy and good fruits, unwavering, without hypocrisy."

— James 3:17 (NASB)

Preface

I didn't realize it at the time, but it started with an argument in our kitchen.

Not yelling, just that quiet tension when both people are sure they're right.

My wife wanted to think, reflect, and pray before deciding. I wanted to make a decision and move on. She listened for God's whisper. I trusted what His Word already said. We were different!

We both loved God deeply, but our ways couldn't have been more different. She led with heart and patience. I led with logic and truth. Both mattered, but we often missed each other.

That difference spilled into every part of life, family choices, church discussions, and even small daily things. **I looked for facts; she looked for feelings**. I wanted clarity; she wanted peace. And more than once, the path to a decision left us both frustrated, even when we agreed in the end.

After one long and emotional church meeting, I said, "The Bible makes this choice simple." She smiled softly and asked, "Maybe. But did anyone consider people's feelings, or how it made them feel?"

That question stayed with me. Although I did not want anyone to know, it created a crisis of doubt about my understanding. My confidence was shaken by my wife's unwavering compassion more than any argument ever could. I began to see how often truth and emotion, wisdom and heart, pull in opposite directions when **God meant them to work together**.

So I started searching ... through scripture, prayer, and a lot of personal reflection. Two years later, I came to realize what I'd been missing: Godly decision-making isn't about speed or emotion. It's about walking the narrow path of balancing God's wisdom with a heart that still feels.

The Narrow Choice grew out of that realization. It offers a Biblical way to bring head and heart together, so each decision leads us closer to Christ. It's not an overnight cure, but if followed, **it's a transformational journey to making decisions you won't regret.** It's one I am still walking.

My hope is simple: that you will join me in the journey and that these pages help you find peace in your choices while leading you to a deeper relationship with God along the way.

Make Decisions
You Won't Regret
A simple, biblical path to clarity and peace

FACTS   FEELINGS

My people are destroyed for lack of knowledge.
— Hosea 4:6

The Narrow Choice

Christian Wisdom
for Decisions You Won't Regret

Introduction: The Decision Dilemma

This book is an invitation to discover how to make decisions as a Christian, not just to learn about decision-making from the Bible, but to live it out every day. You'll find practical ways to sort out the truth and calm your emotions.

You will learn how to make decisions that honor God and bring peace to your life. We'll explore how your feelings and fact-based thinking can work together under God's guidance, rather than fighting against each other.

I must confess, as someone hardwired for facts and logic, I've often overlooked the pull of emotion. But then Scripture gently corrects: "God created mankind in His own image" *(Genesis 1:27, NASB)*. And what do we see consistently in God's character? Emotion: righteous, rich, and real. So, as creations in His image, we come by emotion naturally!

Yet our emotions are corrupted by sin, which science confirms. Psychological research shows that, although we claim to be logical creatures, we often let emotions steer the wheel, especially under duress.

You'd think that when making decisions, facts would win the day. I thought so, too. **Wrong!**

Think about it: Have you ever faced a big decision but felt completely stuck? Why does this struggle between feelings and facts happen when it's time to make a decision? If we are willing to admit it, all of us have had moments when a decision seems out of reach. Why?

The truth is, **we're often afraid of what might happen** after we make a decision. We worry about how things might turn out. That fear can freeze us in place, making it nearly impossible to choose when neither decision feels like a clear win.

The tug-of-war between logic and longing, between fact and feeling, is no stranger to any soul. It's a universal standoff: intellect bracing against emotion, reason wrestling with instinct.

- For believers, **this struggle is more than psychological; it's spiritual.** Should our decisions lean on sheer data or doctrinal rigidity, or is there room for emotion and feelings in the divine equation?

- How does God want us to weigh our options, especially when our hearts whisper one thing while His Word declares another?

These aren't idle musings for ivory tower religious gurus. They hit home in the daily grind. From mundane breakfast dilemmas to high-stakes calls, like whether to end a relationship, take a new job, or downsize our home. And our jobs and church life are not exempt from this either. Whether it's hiring, firing, taking moral stands, or setting a new church budget, life relentlessly demands decisions.

The Premise:

This book is founded on one of the most important decisions a person can make: to follow Jesus as Lord and Savior. Without that connection to God, you may find this book helpful. Still, you may not fully understand or be able to incorporate its guidance.

If you are a Christian, you can skip to the "**In Closing**" page **at the end of this section.** If you do not have that connection to God through Christ, you will still find this book helpful, but I invite you to consider the following:

1. **The Problem:** God is Holy, and we are not because we have sinned. Because our sin separates us from

God, we will suffer physical and eternal spiritual death.

- **Romans 3:23:** *"For all have sinned and fall short of the glory of God."*

- **Romans 6:23:** *"For the wages of sin is death, but the free gift of God is eternal life in Christ Jesus our Lord.*

2. **The Solution:** The penalty for sin is death. But God sent His son, Christ, to take the punishment we deserved by dying on the cross. We accept the solution by confessing (admitting) our sin (imperfections) and calling on Jesus to be Lord of our lives.

   - **(Romans 5:8):** *"But God demonstrates His own love toward us, in that while we were still sinners, Christ died for us."*

   - **Romans 10:9–10:** *"If you confess with your mouth Jesus as Lord, and believe in your heart that God raised Him from the dead, you will be saved."*

   - **Romans 10:13:** *"For everyone who calls on the name of the Lord will be saved."*

3. **The follow-up:** Being a Christian is a lifelong journey, not a weekend retreat. It requires mentoring and fellowship. Connect with a church in your area and attend regularly.

In Closing

James B. Fannin

My prayer and goal for you as you read this book is this:

That you'll uncover how your emotional sensitivity and God-given intellect can work together, yielding decisions that glorify God and ground your life in peace.

This page left blank intentionally

Chapter 1: The Essence of Emotions in Faith

God Feels - And That Changes Everything

When we think of God, adjectives like "all-knowing," "everlasting," and "almighty" spring to mind. We picture the grand cosmic architect reigning in transcendent wisdom. But pause for a moment: how often do we consider that this same God... feels?

Yes, God rejoices. He grieves. He burns with holy anger. He delights with singing *(Zephaniah 3:17),* loves with abandon *(John 3:16),* and grieves with tears (Genesis 6:6). These aren't metaphors; they're revelations. God's emotional life is real, untainted, and foundational to His character.

When He revealed Himself to Moses in *Exodus 34:6–7*, God didn't list His job titles or miracles. He described his emotional makeup as "compassionate," "gracious," "slow to anger," and "abounding in loving kindness." That's not doctrine from a cold distance; that's divine intimacy, where God reveals His character!

Remember, God said in *Genesis 1:26,* "...Let Us make mankind in Our image, according to Our likeness;...". His image and likeness mean that we have His characteristics.

Our emotional capacity isn't a glitch in the design. It's divine engineering. Your joy, sadness, anger, and love all mirror God's emotional DNA, though, admittedly, our mirrors are cracked by sin.

Our Emotions: Beautiful, But Bent

Unlike God's perfect emotional compass, ours often spins erratically. What was once a soul-level GPS pointing toward heaven got knocked out of alignment in the Garden of Eden. When Adam and Eve fell, they didn't just fracture the Garden of Eden; **they fractured everything, including their emotional clarity.**

Take "**fear**". An emotion meant to warn and protect, it now imprisons or stimulates irrational actions. "**Anger**," once a righteous fire for justice, often erupts in selfish rage. Even "**love**," that crown jewel of divine characteristics, can mutate into obsession or manipulation.

Don't delete the file to fix the typo. **Emotions still matter**. They alert us to danger, connect us to others, and motivate righteous action. They are not enemies of faith, but they need to be trained, tamed, and tethered to Christ.

Paul hits this nail squarely: we're to "take every thought captive" to the obedience of Christ *(2 Corinthians 10:5)*. That includes emotional thoughts. Not to deny them, but to disciple them.

The Core Emotions Through a Holy Lens

Psychologists such as Paul Ekman and Robert Plutchik have identified core types of human emotions, including joy, sadness, fear, anger, surprise, disgust, and more nuanced blends like trust and anticipation. **Science ... meet Scripture.**

These are the same emotions we see displayed by God. Since we are made in His image, it is not surprising we have the same emotions. It's just that ours are corrupted, which results in a few feelings unique to humans. For instance, God is never surprised!

Let's walk through a few of these, not as a lab project, but with our minds and Bible open:

- **Joy** – Not the fleeting buzz of happiness, but a Spirit-born resilience *(Galatians 5:22)*. Paul says, "Rejoice in the Lord always" *(Philippians 4:4)*. That's not circumstantial. That's spiritual muscle.

- **Sadness** – Jesus wept *(John 11:35)*. The Man of Sorrows *(Isaiah 53:3)* embraced the hurts of a broken world. Tears aren't a weakness, but windows to God's heart.

- **Fear** – Mentioned more than **500 times** in Scripture, fear is complex. There's the trembling awe before God *(Proverbs 9:10),* and there's the paralyzing dread that blocks faith *(2 Kings 6:15–17)*. One leads to wisdom, the other to worry.

- **Anger** – Righteous when aligned with justice (as with Jesus clearing the temple), but dangerous when left to boil unchecked *(James 1:19–20)*. Be angry, and sin not.

- **Disgust** – God "hates" pride, lying, and injustice *(Proverbs 6:16–19)*. Disgust, when holy, turns us from sin. When warped, it becomes contempt.

- **Trust** – More than emotion, trust is faith in motion. "Trust in the Lord with all your heart And do not lean on your own understanding. ..." *(Proverbs 3:5–6).* It's the soil from which peace grows.

- **Anticipation** – Hope, in biblical terms, isn't wishful thinking; it's confident expectation. "We hope for what we do not see" *(Romans 8:24–25),* but we hope like heirs awaiting their Father's promise.

> **These aren't just feelings, they're sacred echoes. Emotions, when surrendered, point us toward a deeper truth. But left unexamined, they can hijack holy intentions.**

When Emotions Misdirect the Journey

Jeremiah 17:9 delivers a sobering truth: "The heart is more deceitful than all else and desperately sick."

Fear might tell you to stay put when God says, **'Move.'** **Desire** might justify sin. **Guilt** might keep you shackled long after God has forgiven you. **Emotions can't always be trusted to lead.**

Think of David and Bathsheba. Lust clouded his vision and torched his *integrity (2 Samuel 11)*. Think of the disciples panicking in a storm while Jesus slept *(Mark 4:38)*. Or Elijah, curled up under a tree, begging to die (1 Kings 19), forgetting that just days earlier, he'd called down fire from heaven.

Each moment is raw emotion. Unfiltered and corrupted by sin. It confirms... humans have fallen from the perfect balance God originally created. And a reminder: unchecked emotion is a poor compass.

Translation? Your gut feeling might be wrong!

Emotions Are Signs, Not Steering Wheels

They can tell you something important, but shouldn't decide your route.

- Fear says, "Look out!"
- Wisdom replies, "Let's verify before we panic."
- Anger cries out, "This isn't right!"
- Truth answers, "Let's address it with justice, not vengeance."
- Joy beams, "This is good!"
- Discernment whispers, "Is it good in God's eyes, or just yours?"

- Compassion yearns to know, "Am I honoring God's commands; will it bring someone closer to God, or does it just make you feel better?"

Jesus modeled this balance flawlessly. He wept, got angry, rejoiced, grieved, but never once did His emotions override obedience. He felt everything and still chose the cross *(Matthew 26:39)*.

> **Think of emotions as road signs, not the steering wheel!**

Becoming Emotionally Intelligent … Spiritually

What today's psychologists call "emotional intelligence[1]" Scripture simply calls wisdom.

Jesus, our perfect model, showed us how to live alert to emotion yet anchored in truth. He used empathy without enabling. He confronted without harshness. He navigated every relational landmine with clarity and compassion.

Want to grow in this biblical version of emotional intelligence? Start here:

- **Self-Awareness** – Know what you're feeling and why.
- **Self-Control** – Don't be ruled by those feelings.
- **Empathy** – Tune in to others without losing your center.
- **Wise Interaction** – Speak truth in love. Always.

This is not emotional suppression. It's spiritual maturity.

Next Step: Knowledge vs. Emotion

In the next chapter, we'll look at how our emotions can sometimes mislead us. We will see how God's truth serves as an anchor that guides our feelings without ignoring them.

You'll see how Jesus handled His own feelings without letting them control His obedience. You'll begin to understand how the knowledge of God's Word helps us rise above fear and walk with confidence in His promises.

This page left blank intentionally

Chapter 2: Knowledge vs. Emotion: A Biblical Analysis

When the Heart Plays Tricks

> "The heart is deceitful above all things and desperately sick; who can understand it?" *(Jeremiah 17:9, NASB)*

That verse doesn't politely hint at emotional unreliability; it shouts a divine warning. The human heart, Scripture says, isn't a neutral decision-maker. Not unsurprisingly, this bias is confirmed by psychologists. It bends, twists, and exaggerates. It's beautiful, yes, but it's also deceitful.

In the Hebrew world, "**heart**" wasn't just where emotions lived; it was the command center of the soul: thoughts, affections, motives, and decisions all intertwined. So, when Jeremiah calls it "deceitful," he means the ***whole inner life*** **is susceptible to misdirection**.

It's the old game: ***Feel first, then justify with reason***. Our emotions leap ahead, and our intellect scrambles to catch up, drafting arguments to defend decisions we've already emotionally committed to.

- "I probably shouldn't splurge on this, but after the week I've had, I deserve it."

- "I know, I should forgive her, but what she did hurt way too much."

- "This relationship isn't ideal, but what if no one else comes along?"

> *We dress our feelings in the clothing of reason and call it discernment. But it's really deception, stitched together in the back room of our desires.*

Why Knowledge Isn't Optional

"My people are destroyed for lack of knowledge." *(Hosea 4:6)*

God never intended for His people to live on emotional instinct. The Bible abounds with calls to seek knowledge, wisdom, and understanding, not just academically but also relationally. The Hebrew term *"yada"* means "**to know**." In biblical terms, "to know" is different from what we usually think it means. In biblical terms, it implies intimacy, connection, and depth.

This isn't head knowledge that just bounces around in our brain; it's truth absorbed into the bloodstream of decision-making.

The Proverbs tell us:

- "The heart of the discerning acquires knowledge…" *(Proverbs 18:15)*
- "Wisdom is supreme, get wisdom. And with all your acquiring, get understanding." *(Proverbs 4:7)*

- And Paul urges us to "grow in the grace and knowledge of our Lord" *(2 Peter 3:18)*. Not just *grace*, but also *knowledge*.

So, what does this look like when emotions flare? It means tying every gut feeling to something firmer than instinct. It means questioning our emotions to ensure they align with the facts and what we know.

> *Are the emotions justified, or are they overriding our knowledge? In the absence of knowledge or facts, we must have restraint. Otherwise, emotions will rise because it's the only thing we have to focus on.*

Jesus: The Masterclass in Emotional Clarity

Jesus didn't ignore emotions; He mastered them. He wept over Jerusalem *(Luke 19:41)*, felt sorrow in Gethsemane *(Matthew 26:38)*, burned with anger in the temple *(John 2:15–17)*, and rejoiced in the Holy Spirit *(Luke 10:21)*.

But never once did emotion hijack His obedience.

In the desert, when Satan tempted Him with shortcuts, emotional appeals, hunger, ego, and power, Jesus replied, "It is written…" *(Matthew 4)*. Truth trumped temptation. Scripture outweighed impulse.

And in Gethsemane, He cried out in agony, 'Let this cup pass from Me," yet surrendered with, 'Not as I will, but as

You will" *(Matthew 26:39)*. Emotion acknowledged. Truth obeyed. That's our model.

> *Jesus never silenced His emotions, but He never allowed them to silence God's will.*

Fear: The Master Manipulator

If emotion had a ringmaster, its name would be *fear*. It masquerades as caution, wisdom, even humility, but often, it's just control in disguise. The Ringmaster in a three-ring circus directs our attention to what he wants us to watch, see, and feel. He controls our experience by getting us to overlook whatever else may be happening in the other rings.

Fear, like the Ringmaster, doesn't just nudge us; it commands us to pay attention. It tells us:

- "Stay where it's safe."
- "Don't look there .. look here!"
- "They might reject you if you ask questions."
- "They might get mad if you don't go along."
- "Focus on your feelings."
- "If you feel strongly, just follow your feelings."
- "What if God doesn't come through?"
- "God will be angry if you bother Him with small stuff."

Scripture isn't shy about addressing fear.

Scripture mentions "*fear*" or its synonym "*afraid*" **more than 540 times.** If you expand that to include anxious, frightened, or other closely related emotions, **it totals over 700 times**.

Yet, "**Hell**," in all its derivative forms ... is mentioned less than 25 times, and "**Redeem**" or "**Redeemer**" ... in all variations and forms is mentioned about 100 times.

> *Both "Hell" and "Redeemer" are fundamental biblical and theological concepts in Christianity. Yet "fear" is mentioned up to 20 times more often!*

This isn't coincidental. God understands that fear is an important emotion in the human experience. The sheer frequency with which fear is part of the biblical story suggests that God recognizes it **as the root cause of human hesitation**, rebellion, poor choices, and paralysis.

(1)Fear is likely the primary emotional force behind poor decisions. Yet, when we allow fear, much like the ringmaster, to direct our attention to see and feel *only* what it wants, it becomes nearly impossible to make wise, biblically informed, faith-based decisions.

Consider Elisha's servant. Aside from Elisha, he was likely the "top dog" and ran the place. As was customary for the chief servant, he was also probably responsible for security. He was a competent and confident manager of the prophet's school.

Yet, he awakened one morning and saw only the army surrounding the compound and at the gate, not the chariots of fire on the hills *(2 Kings 6:15–17)*. **The servant was afraid**. His emotion was so great that he was effectively paralyzed. He was unable to think clearly. Despite his position, he didn't know what to do. Fear had narrowed his vision.

On the other hand, Elisha was not afraid. **Why?**

> *Elisha had knowledge that the servant did not.*

Elisha saw God's chariots of fire all around them, standing at the ready. The servant's lack of this knowledge, which Elisha possessed, allowed emotion to overcome him and hide the reality of the moment. So Elisha prayed, "Lord, open his eyes."

That's what we need, eyes opened to reality that can carry us beyond our emotional fog. So the antidote to fear, to emotion, isn't bravado, or pretending it does not exist.

It's not *"feel the fear and do it anyway."* It's not panic and paralysis! It's **knowledge,** facts, specifically, the knowledge and fact of God's unchanging character.

- **His faithfulness** *(Lamentations 3:23)* – "They are new every morning; Great is Your faithfulness."

- **His nearness** *(Psalm 34:18)* – "The Lord is near to the brokenhearted and saves those who are crushed in spirit."

- **His power** *(Ephesians 3:20)* – "Now to Him who is able to do far more abundantly beyond all that we ask or think, according to the power that works within us,"

- **His promises** *(Romans 8:28) – "And we know that God causes all things to work together for good to those who love God, to those who are called according to His purpose."*

Praying for Open Eyes

Our need for the knowledge of God's Word should make Elisha's prayer ours, too: **"Lord, open my eyes."**

Open my eyes to:

- **Your presence** when I feel abandoned – "... for He Himself has said, "I will never desert you, nor will I ever abandon you,". *(Hebrews 13:5)*

- **Your provision** when my resources seem scarce – "And my God will supply all your needs according to His riches in glory in Christ Jesus." *(Philippians 4:19)*

- **Your plan** when everything feels off-course – "For as the heavens are higher than the earth, So are My ways higher than your ways And My thoughts than your thoughts." *(Isaiah 55:9)*

- **Your peace** when my heart is in chaos – "Peace I leave you, My peace I give you; not as the world gives, do I give to you. Do not let your hearts be troubled, nor fearful." *(John 14:27)*

This kind of spiritual insight doesn't come from self-talk or ignoring your emotions. It comes from immersion in the Word, communion with the Spirit, and wise counsel from trusted believers.

> *Truth, when illuminated by the Spirit, cuts through emotional fog like sunlight slicing morning mist.*

Next Step: Heart and Mind in Relationships

We don't make decisions in a vacuum. Emotions get amplified ... and complicated when others are involved. In relationships, our choices aren't just affected by *our* emotions but also by *theirs*.

In the next chapter, we'll explore how Scripture equips us to respond with our heart and mind engaged as we face the emotional dynamics that influence our decisions in family, friendships, and church life.

Chapter 3: Emotions in Relationships

The Family Furnace: Where Emotion Meets Decision

If you want to know how emotions impact decision-making, just observe a family under stress. One child's rebellion, a looming financial strain, or an unexpected relocation can turn even the most rational household into an emotional wildfire.

Why? Because family touches our core identity. These are the people we love fiercely ... and the ones who trigger us the most.

The decision on how to discipline a teenager can leave the child feeling uncertain or insecure and leave adults feeling regret, resentment, or anger.

Conversations and decisions about elder care often expose long-buried resentment, guilt, fear of angering the subject elder, or fear of making the wrong decision.

Financial decisions, especially when resources are tight, can amplify feelings of fear, blame, or shame.

But emotions in family life aren't liabilities; they're signals. They reveal what matters most. Still, they must be handled with wisdom, not just a reactive approach driven solely by feelings and emotions.

Ephesians 6:4 offers a guidepost: *"Fathers, do not provoke your children to anger, but bring them up in the discipline and instruction of the Lord."* That's not just about parenting; it's about emotional intelligence.

> **Discipline, yes, but not in rage. Instruction, yes, but wrapped in compassion.**

Whether you're choosing where to live, how to spend, or how to guide your children, here's a path:

1. **Acknowledge emotions:** "I can see this move feels scary for you."

2. **Unpack the facts:** "Let's look at our finances and the job offer together."

3. **Root decisions in Scripture:** "What does God say about trust, stewardship, and sacrifice?"

4. **Pray together:** "Let's ask God for unity and wisdom."

> **With emotions and truth guided by scripture, even a family can realize that difficult decisions become moments of trust and stronger relationships.**

Emotional Intelligence in the Body of Christ

Church is a spiritual home, but it's still filled with human beings. This means that decisions there, too, are often driven by emotion.

Think about church life:
- A shift in ministry focus.
- A staffing change.
- Budget allocations and priorities.
- A budget shortfall.
- Disagreements or conflicts between members.
- These aren't just logistical decisions. They're emotionally charged environments. And they require emotional intelligence rooted in the Spirit.

Emotional intelligence, biblically speaking, means:
- **Self-awareness** – *"Search me, O God..." (Psalm 139:23-24)*
- **Self-regulation** – *"Like a city broken into is the person without control over his spirit." (Proverbs 25:28)*
- **Empathy** – *"Rejoice with those who rejoice; weep with those who weep." (Romans 12:15)*
- **Wise relationships** – *"Speak the truth in love." (Ephesians 4:15)*

Jesus was the perfect example of this over and over. He wept with grieving sisters at Lazarus's tomb *(John 11:35)*. He calmed panicked disciples during an angry storm at sea *(Mark 4:39)*.

33

He led with compassion when correcting a woman caught in sin *(John 8:11)*. Jesus never dismissed emotions ... but He never let them derail the truth of God's love and character.

When Other People's Feelings Hijack Our Decisions

Let's be honest, we've all made decisions just to keep the peace, avoid conflict, or stay in someone's good graces.

- You say "yes" to a favor that drains you because you fear disappointing them.
- You silence the truth because you're scared of someone's anger.
- You bend your values because you crave a feeling of belonging.

Not all emotional influence is bad. Jesus was "moved with compassion" when He saw that the crowds following Him were stressed and depressed *(Matthew 9:36)*. His disciples had seen Jesus' works. They knew His power to heal, comfort, and restore.

And the disciples, no doubt, knew and felt as Jesus did. Seeing the despair in the eyes of the crowds as they mingled with them must have stirred strong emotions. **They almost certainly suggested to Jesus that he do something,** or at least, strongly suspected He would do something "unexpected" to relieve their distress.

Jesus did do something ... unexpected! His compassion led him to plead for more workers to spread the Gospel. It did not lead to hysterical emotions and rash actions. Jesus saw the bigger picture and knew God's long-term plans. In other words, **knowledge** informed His actions.

> *This action, this model of behavior, is an example of how we must allow the Holy Spirit to restrain our knee-jerk response. It teaches us to let the Holy Spirit guide our responses rather than reacting to other people's feelings.*

It reminds us to trust the wisdom God gives us in His Word, rather than letting other people's emotions push aside what the Bible clearly says.

For example, think of Aaron. Pressured by the people, he gave them a golden calf (Exodus 32). Or Pilate, who washed his hands while handing Jesus over to be crucified ... because he **feared** the crowd (Matthew 27:24).

Romans 12:2 reminds us, *"Do not be conformed to this world, but be transformed by the renewing of your mind..."* Translation? Don't let public emotion override personal conviction.

Here's a way to work through these circumstances:

- **Identify it**: "I feel pressure to agree, but is this God's path or just people-pleasing?"
- **Ground it**: "What does Scripture say about this?"

35

- **Speak truth gently**: "I care about you deeply, but I choose to make this decision based on what I believe God is telling me."

Holy Communication in Heated Moments

Communication isn't just about giving information. **It's the meeting place of emotion**, intention, and truth. In emotionally charged conversations, what we say *and how we say it* can either defuse the tension or ignite the fire.

James 1:19 offers a master class in divine communication: ... "be quick to hear, slow to speak, and slow to anger; ..."

Let's break that down:

- **Quick to hear** – Active listening, not just waiting to talk.
- **Slow to speak** – Resisting the urge to react.
- **Slow to anger** – Allowing the Spirit to filter your emotions before they explode.

Other golden anchors for emotional communication:

- **Truth + Love** (*Ephesians 4:15*) -- "but speaking the truth in love..."

- **Gracious tone** (*Colossians 4:6*) –"Your speech must always be with grace, as though seasoned with salt, so that you will know how you should respond to each person."

- **Building up** (*Ephesians 4:29*) – "Let no unwholesome word come out of your mouth, but if there is any good word for edification according to the need of the moment, say that, so that it will give grace to those who hear."

- **Soft answers** (*Proverbs 15:1*) – "A gentle answer turns away wrath, but a harsh word stirs up anger."

Whether you're speaking with a spouse, a small group leader, or a friend who has wounded you, these principles form a communication foundation that promotes truth while honoring emotions.

Reconciliation: The Gospel in Decision Form

Some of the most powerful decisions we make are the ones that rebuild broken bridges. Restoration after relational rupture requires more than emotion. **It demands clarity, grace, and structure.**

Jesus lays it out in **Matthew 18:15-17**. Go privately. Bring witnesses if needed. Involve the church if it escalates. That's not bureaucracy, but divine wisdom for emotional chaos.

Forgiveness, too, isn't merely a feeling ... it's a decision. It must be a conscious decision to relinquish the right to retaliate. It must be a commitment to cancel the emotional debt. It's not always instant, but it starts with intention and persistence.

- Acknowledge the hurt.
- Clarify the offense.

- Confess, forgive, or both.

- Rebuild trust with **consistency**, not just apologies.

Jesus didn't just *preach* reconciliation. He **embodied** it ... stretching out His arms on a cross to settle the greatest conflict of all.

.

Chapter 4: Balancing Heart and Mind

Five Anchors for Faithful Decisions

The Christian life isn't a tug-of-war between the head and the heart; it's a dance. And like all dances, someone must lead. For us, it must be God's Spirit guiding our emotions and our understanding of God's Word into harmony.

Every aspect of life requires us to make decisions. Jobs, school, teaching, parenting, relationships, driving, planning, and finances **all require conscious decisions**. Even getting up in the morning is a decision.

You get the message. We are required to make thousands of decisions every day. Some are easy, even automatic, no-brainers. Some, not so much.

I have studied scripture since I was 16, including while in college. After decades of researching the Bible while seeking to live for the Lord, I see **five timeless principles** that are like giant, towering stones at the foot of a desert mountain.

Despite centuries of blinding sandstorms and howling winds, these stones stand unmoved, rising above the plain like giant monuments.

> *Like the stones, these five principles rise above the plain for all to see – solid, trustworthy, and still standing after the storm.*

I believe these are the beacons that guide us and help us navigate the swirl of decision-making across all areas.

1. Emotions Are Indicators, Not Instructors

> Like a city that is broken into and without walls, so is a person who has no self-control over his spirit. *(Proverbs 25:28)*

Emotions are real. Powerful. Designed by God. **But they were never meant to be the captain of the ship.** They're more like the weather vane, helpful for reading directions, but not to be confused with the compass.

So, what do we do with our emotions?

- **Identify them**: "Lord, I feel nervous about this."
- **Trace them**: "Where is this fear coming from? Is it rooted in past failure? Future uncertainty?"
- **Surrender them**: "I give this to You. Replace my fear with Your peace. Take my pride, and fill me with Your grace."

> *Remember ... emotions are real. Powerful. Designed by God. But they were never meant to be the captain of the ship. They're more like the weather vane, helpful for reading directions, but not to be confused with the compass.*

2. Knowledge Grounds the Storm

> The mind of the intelligent seeks knowledge, But the mouth of fools feeds on foolishness. *(Proverbs 15:14)*

There's no virtue in blind emotion or hollow sentimentality. **God calls us to pursue understanding with intention.** It's not faithless to research, study, or ask hard questions. It's wisdom.

Balanced decision-making means:

- **Looking at Scripture** for timeless principles.
- **Gathering real facts**, not just opinions or fears.
- **Listening to the testimonies** of those who've walked this road before.

> *Wisdom isn't anti-emotion. It just insists that truth holds the steering wheel while feelings ride in the passenger seat.*

3. Prayer: The Heart's Reset Button

"But if any of you lacks wisdom, let him ask of God, who gives to all generously and without reproach, and it will be given to him." *(James 1:5)*

When Solomon had the golden chance to ask God for anything, he didn't ask for riches, fame, or long life. **He asked for wisdom** *(1 Kings 3:9)*. And God was so pleased with the request that He gave Solomon the wisdom he asked for, wealth beyond measure, and every other material blessing one could want.

Prayer opens that same vault of divine wisdom to us.

> *Prayer isn't just about "feeling better", it's about recalibration. It realigns your will with God's. It cools hot emotions. It spotlights wrong motives. It slows you down to heaven's pace.*

4. Speak Less. Listen More. Then Decide.

"... Now everyone must be quick to hear, slow to speak, and slow to anger;" *(James 1:19)*

Our culture idolizes quick replies and snap decisions. But biblical decision-making is countercultural. It slows down. It listens deeply. It waits for clarity. It creates space for the Spirit to speak before we do.

In heated decisions, especially where people and emotions are involved, try this:

- **Wait** before responding.

- **Ask** clarifying questions.

- **Pray** before pressing send or speaking up.

- **Test** your words before releasing them into the world.

> *God is rarely in a hurry but always on time.*

5. Trust God: Even When the Fog Doesn't Lift

"Do not be anxious about anything... and the peace of God... will guard your hearts and your minds in Christ Jesus." (Philippians 4:6-7)

Peace isn't the absence of tension, it's the presence of God in the tension. We see this when we look at the word "**anxious**" in the original language. It is not the same word we typically associate with the modern-day words, "**anxious**" or "**worry**."

Instead, it has a Greek prefix that means "**hyper**." It is the same prefix we use with familiar words such as "**hyperactive**" or "**hyperventilate**", and as a verb when we say, "**Don't be so hyper**."

In Greek, the prefix, as in modern English, means being overly excited, excessive, or frenetic. So, in this context, it **does not mean** the absence of anxiety, concern, or worry.

We are human, and as humans, it would be practically impossible not to think about something that concerns us. **Instead, our trust in God keeps us from being overly concerned. (i.e, hyper!)**

It gives us peace that, despite our inability to see past an issue, God sees past it and knows the outcome. Further, He will give us the courage and ability to accept the outcome, knowing it will work out according to God's plan.

With that in mind, this verse means **don't be "hyper."** It means don't be overly concerned or worried.

> *This understanding dispels the notion that we must have peace before we make a decision.*

On the other hand, it does not mean we should rush ahead. Instead, it means we should use the resources God has given us to evaluate the situation using the intellect, knowledge, resources, and abilities He has given us.

You may not have 100% certainty of the correct answer before taking the next step. You might still feel nervous or unsure. But consider this:

- If your choice fits with what the Bible teaches
- You've prayed about it
- God has not shown you it's wrong
- Wise Christian people agree it's good

Then go ahead and trust God to lead you. God will honor your diligence and trust with a peace that comes from your trust and confidence that God is in control.

> *Yes, we want it. But peace doesn't always precede action; instead, it often follows trust.*

When we understand this verse, we realize:

Trust isn't a feeling; it's a choice.

Peace isn't the absence of tension; it's the presence of God in the tension. When we trust God, the concern doesn't go away. Instead, we turn the outcome over to God.

It is when we recognize that He is both able and willing to carry us through an uncertain moment to accomplish His will, if only we put our trust in Him.

Why Prayer Deserves More Than a Checkbox

Prayer is not the backup plan. It's not a prelude. It's the foundation.

When we ask God for wisdom, He doesn't roll His eyes. He leans in. He listens. He responds, not always how we expect, but always with generosity and grace.

Jesus didn't just teach prayer; He lived it. Before choosing His disciples, He spent the entire night in prayer (Luke 6:12).

Before the cross, He prayed with blood-sweating agony (Luke 22:44). Prayer isn't passive ... it's spiritual warfare, surrender, intimacy, and clarity all at once.

Want clarity in your next big decision?

- Begin with prayer.
- Linger in prayer.
- Listen in prayer.
- Wait in prayer.

Then move forward with confidence that you've included the only opinion that matters most.

Next Steps or Next Chapter?

We've covered a lot of ground here, anchoring emotions, embracing knowledge, kneeling in prayer, quieting our speech, and trusting God when logic runs dry.

But how does all this look in real-life decisions? How do we harmonize this blend of emotions and God's wisdom when money is tight, career shifts loom, love confuses us, compassion overwhelms, or ministry calls stretch us beyond our comfort zone?

If you're ready, let's dive into **Chapter 5: Balanced Decision-Making in Real Life ...** where theology meets Monday morning!

Chapter 5: Balanced Decision-Making in Real Life

Finances: When Fear and Faith Collide

Money isn't just numbers; it's emotional. It whispers promises of safety. It shouts warnings of lack. It fuels pride. It stirs shame. And yet, how we handle money says a lot about who we trust.

> *Jesus knew this, which is why He spoke more about money than about heaven or hell. He knew its power to shape our choices and our hearts.*

Two extremes often plague financial decisions:

- **Fear-based hoarding** – We stockpile, save, and say no to generosity because we fear the bottom might fall out.

- **Desire-driven spending** – We chase emotional highs through purchases, masking discontent with Amazon boxes and clearance tags.

Both are distortions. Both are emotional. And both ignore biblical stewardship.

Proverbs 21:5 teaches, "The plans of the diligent lead surely to advantage, but everyone who is hasty comes surely to poverty."

In other words ... PLAN. Don't panic. Don't act impulsively.

Balanced financial decision-making means:

- **Recognizing the emotions** behind our spending (fear, pride, envy, comfort).

- **Building systems** that reflect biblical principles, budgets, giving plans, and accountability partners.

- **Asking the hard questions**: "Is this purchase about purpose or about proving something?"

> *God isn't trying to take from you: He's trying to lead you. When you surrender your wallet to Him, you'll find freedom that money can never buy.*

Careers: When Calling and Comfort Clash

Career decisions aren't just professional, they're deeply spiritual. They touch identity, purpose, provision, and direction. That's why they're so emotional.

Some play it safe, sticking with what's familiar because it feels secure. Others chase passion, leaping before looking. But Scripture invites us to another way: *calling.*

Ephesians 2:10 says we are "created in Christ Jesus for good works, which God prepared beforehand." **That means your career isn't just a paycheck ... it's a platform.** A pulpit in disguise.

How do we discern wisely?

- **Assess your gifts** – What do others affirm in you? What work feels life-giving?

- **Assess the needs** – What gaps do you see in your workplace, industry, or community?

- **Assess your heart** – Are you running toward a mission or running from discomfort?

Balanced career decisions are less about climbing ladders and more about aligning with God's assignment. And don't rush. Small steps, volunteering, mentoring, and testing ideas often lead to divine clarity.

Relationships: When Emotions Run Deep

Few decisions carry more emotional weight than those involving people, dating, marriage, parenting, and friendships. Love is powerful, but love unmoored from wisdom can shipwreck lives.

Jesus tells us to love with heart, soul, and **mind** (Matthew 22:37). **Not to cool love's fire, but to keep it from burning everything down.**

When dating or discerning marriage:

- Don't confuse chemistry with covenant readiness.

- Observe character over time, not just connection in the moment.

- Ask: "Does this relationship point me to Jesus, or pull me away?"

In parenting:

- Emotion-only parenting becomes either overly permissive or overly harsh.

- Wisdom-based parenting sets boundaries in love and explains consequences with grace.

- Discipline without emotional clarity wounds. Emotion without structure weakens.

And in friendships:

- Discern whether a friendship feeds your spirit or just your ego.

- Ask: "Am I choosing friends who sharpen me (Proverbs 27:17) or sedate my convictions?"

- When love and wisdom walk hand in hand, relationships flourish without foolishness.

Ministry: When Passion Must Partner With Purpose

To be clear, every Christian, not just the pastor and church staff, has a ministry.

God saved you as a whole person, and He does not view your life as divided into secular or religious parts.

As a Christian, your ministry may be anywhere, in any part of your life. You may even minister to more than one group.

Your calling may be to volunteer in church, care for neighbors, nurture and witness to co-workers, friends, family, or even strangers you may meet socially. Wherever it is, remember that just because something stirs your heart doesn't mean it's your assignment. Ministry decisions must balance Spirit-led passion with prayer-soaked discernment.

Romans 12:1–2 speaks to this: Offer your whole life to God, be transformed by renewing your mind, and then you'll **know** His will, what is good, pleasing, and perfect.

Before diving into any ministry opportunity:

- **Ask:** "Does this match my gifting or just my guilt?" For example, some may not be good teachers but are great encouragers and relationship builders. Don't let the emotion of guilt lead you to poor decisions.

- **Consider:** "Am I being stretched in faith, or pulled beyond grace?" For example, should I give money to someone I know who is struggling because of habitual reckless spending, hoping (faith) they have learned their lesson, or not?

- **Evaluate:** "Will this decision deepen my walk or dilute my priorities?" For example, should I accept a volunteer committee position even though I have family (children's sports) responsibilities, travel 30% of the time, and already serve on another committee?

Even Jesus walked away from crowds to stay aligned with His mission (Mark 1:38). Your personal ministry isn't about doing everything; it's about doing the *right* thing at the *right* time with the *right* heart. That's where emotions must give way to spirit-led decision-making.

> **Remember that just because something stirs your heart doesn't mean it's your assignment.**

Health: Trusting God, Taking Action

Health decisions often swing between extremes:

- "God will heal me. I don't need medicine."

- "The doctor said it, so I'll obey, even if my spirit isn't at peace."

Biblical stewardship means honoring God with our bodies (1 Corinthians 6:19–20). That includes both **trusting God fully** and **using wisdom faithfully**.

Consider:

- **Preventive habits**: Do they reflect fear, laziness, or discipline?

- **Medical treatments**: Are you prayerfully considering them, or just reacting?

- **Mental health**: Are you treating the soul, body, and mind as one integrated creation?

A balanced approach may mean medication, prayer, therapy, Scripture, rest, **and** repentance. God uses all of it when He holds the reins.

Reflection: Pause Before You Proceed

Before you turn the page, consider this:

- What recent decision did you make primarily from emotion?

- What role did Scripture, prayer, and counsel play?

- What would it look like to revisit that decision with both heart and head engaged?

Emotions are not the enemy. But neither are they the authority.

> *When feelings rise, facts whisper, and fear shouts ... turn down the volume of the world and lean into the still small voice that never leads you astray.*

This page left blank intentionally.

Chapter 6: Teaching Future Generations

Wisdom Is Inherited—But Only If Modeled

Have you ever watched a child mimic a parent without even realizing it? The way they fold their arms or repeat a phrase you didn't even know you said, often. They're watching, learning, absorbing.

> *Children model what they see and hear. And generally, the model they learn in childhood follows them into adulthood, subconsciously guiding their behavior even as adults.*

This modeling process was never more evident to me than with my five-year-old grandson's response after being corrected by his mother.

She advised there would be consequences if he continued to make bad decisions. His response was, " I'll take that under consideration." Where does a five-year-old learn to say something like that? ... Naturally, he learned from his mom and dad!

Although the story is cute, it is also serious! It leads to the question, **what decision model will they learn from you?**

Deuteronomy 6:6–7 tells us to "impress [God's commands] on your children. Talk about them when you sit at home and when you walk along the road..."
In other words, model it. Live it. Integrate it.

Kids don't just inherit faith through Sunday School or Bible memory—**they catch it by watching us make everyday decisions.**

Not just the big ones—house buying, job changes, who we marry—but the small ones: how we respond to stress, budget, and speak when we're frustrated.

They notice the way you model your decision-making:

- Do you pause and pray before deciding?

- Do you talk about God's Word when making a choice?

- Do you own up to bad decisions and learn out loud?

Wisdom doesn't happen by accident. It's handed down—on purpose.

Let Them Hear You Think

Children aren't born knowing how to weigh emotions against truth. That's something we must teach— not only by instruction but by *demonstration*.

Next time you face a decision—even something simple—try thinking aloud.

- "I'm excited about this offer, but I want to make sure I'm not being impulsive."

- "Let's check what Scripture says about how we treat others."

- "I'm nervous about this, so I want to pray before we decide."

Verbalizing your process shows that emotions are real but not rulers. That God's Word matters. That prayer isn't a ritual—it's a lifeline.

Admit Mistakes. Let Them Watch You Grow.

Kids don't need perfect examples—they need honest ones.

Some of the most impactful moments you'll ever give your children happen when you own a poor decision:

- "I yelled today because I was stressed, not because you deserved that tone. That was wrong."

- "I rushed into that purchase without praying first. I regret it. Let's fix it together."

Humility teaches. Vulnerability trains. When they see you grow, they learn how to grow, too.

Teach in Layers: Age-Appropriate Training

Wisdom training isn't one-size-fits-all. It grows with them.

- Preschoolers need limited choices to learn basic decision-making. "Do you want the red shirt or the blue shirt?" Even this teaches: your choice carries weight.

- Elementary kids can understand trade-offs and consequences. Introduce Scripture gently. "Let's ask what Jesus might want in this situation."

- Middle schoolers begin wrestling with tensions between emotion and truth. Don't fix their decisions—walk through them. "How do you feel? Now what do we know?"

Teens are ready for deeper application. Introduce the full decision-making framework:

- Balance emotion with wisdom.

- Seek knowledge and spiritual discernment.

- Pray.

- Slow down before reacting.

- Trust God even in uncertainty.

One family created "Decision Journals" for their teens—every big decision required writing down the emotions involved, the Scripture that spoke to it, and what they ultimately chose. It became a spiritual record of their growing maturity.

Build a Home Where Wisdom Is Normal

Some families pass down recipes, traditions, or financial advice. We're called to pass down wisdom. And that takes intentional culture.

Here's how to cultivate it:

- Host family decision meetings: Even young children can observe how decisions are prayed over, facts gathered, and unity pursued.

- Use Scripture like a compass: When you're stuck, say, "Let's see what the Bible might say about this." Memorize key verses together (like Proverbs 3:5–6).

- Celebrate wise choices: Don't just praise good outcomes affirm wise processes. "You thought that through carefully. That honors God."

- Debrief poor decisions without shame: "That didn't turn out well. What can we learn from it for next time?"

- Challenge cultural lies: The world says, "Follow your heart." You say, "Let's check if the heart is pointing north."

Mentor Outside the Walls of Your Home

Wisdom isn't just for your household—it's for the Church Body.

Paul instructed Titus that older believers are to teach the younger (*Titus 2*). That includes how to think, feel, and decide in Christ.

If you're a youth leader, teach emotional intelligence with biblical boundaries.

If you're a pastor, model vulnerability in your decision-making stories.

If you're retired, mentor young adults not just in finances or marriage but in how to weigh God's voice above all.

One older man at church started a monthly "Wisdom Circle"—a casual lunch where younger men could ask questions about jobs, dating, conflict, and more. His only credential? ***A life full of both bad and good decisions—handed back to God in surrender.***

Break the Cycle, Build a Legacy

Some families inherit more than heirlooms—they inherit *patterns* of poor choices. Anger-led decisions. Financial recklessness. Emotional manipulation. Silence instead of confrontation.

But the gospel breaks chains.

"If anyone is in Christ, he is a new creation..." *(2 Corinthians 5:17)*. That includes how we decide.

Start by identifying old cycles:

- Do you run from decisions or rush into them?

- Are you overly influenced by others' emotions?

- Is fear the loudest voice in the room?

- Then, name them. Repent of them. And replace them with something holy:

- Thoughtful decision-making.

- Biblical anchoring.

- Emotional maturity.

- Relational honesty.

God can take a long family line of reactive choices and start a new story—with you. You modeling Biblical, spirit-led emotional intelligence in your decision making, can be the guiding light to that new story.

Want to Build a Family of Decision-Makers? Start Today.

Don't wait for the next big family decision. Begin now:

- Let your kids see you pause and pray.

- Tell the truth about your emotions.

- Celebrate wisdom when you see it.

- Correct without shame.

- Normalize listening for God's voice.

Your ceiling of spiritual maturity can become your children's floor. And that is a legacy worth leaving.

Chapter 7: Conclusion: Embracing the ...

End! ... But This Isn't the End ...

It's the Beginning! By now, you've walked through the challenges and rewards of decision-making. You've seen how emotions, without the framework of God's wisdom, can mislead. How knowledge, without grace, can become cold. And how God invites us to strive toward the perfect balance of emotions and knowledge we had in the Garden of Eden before we were corrupted.

We won't get there perfectly in this life. But we can live with fewer regrets about our decisions while embracing God's mercy and love.

You've learned not to fear your feelings but to guide them. Not to dismiss your thoughts but to surrender them. Most of all, you've seen how both facts and feelings find their proper place under the Lordship of Jesus Christ.

> *But let's be clear: balanced decision-making isn't a one-time achievement. It's a lifelong journey. One marked by humility, repentance, growth, and grace upon grace.*

Growth Is Not Linear

Some days, you'll make decisions with crystal clarity, truth glowing like a lighthouse. On other days, your emotions will cloud the sky, and Scripture may seem quiet.

That's okay.

- God doesn't demand perfection. He asks for progress. And He promises that "He who began a good work in you will carry it on to completion" (*Philippians 1:6*).

- So, celebrate the small wins:
  - The time you paused to pray before speaking.
  - The moment you admitted, "I don't know yet," instead of pretending.
  - The time you chose Scripture over impulse or humility over impulsive reaction.

These are holy milestones. Mark them. Thank God for them.

When You Fall, Fall Into Grace

You'll get it wrong sometimes.

You'll let fear win. You'll speak from anger. You'll ignore wise counsel.

And when that happens, don't spiral into shame. Remember the cross. Remember the Savior who was tempted in every way, yet without sin, who now intercedes for you.

Get up.

Ask forgiveness from God and others.

Learn what you can, and walk forward with even more clarity than before.

Keep Walking: You're Not Alone

You're part of something bigger. A family of faith, all learning together how to listen, trust, and follow the Shepherd's voice.

- Lean on:

  - **The Word** – A lamp for your feet and a light for your path (*Psalm 119:105*).

  - **The Spirit** – The Counselor who teaches and reminds you of truth (*John 14:26*).

  - **The Church** – A body of believers to sharpen and support you (*Hebrews 10:24–25*).

You're never meant to make decisions in isolation. You were made for community, accountability, and encouragement. Keep showing up. Keep asking questions. Keep seeking.

Your Next Right Step

You don't need to have the whole path figured out.

Just the next right step.

So ... what is it?

Is there a decision you've been avoiding or a conversation you need to revisit?

A financial shift you've sensed God prompting?

A boundary to draw? A call to make? A prayer to return to?

Whatever it is, take that step today. Not in fear. Not in pride. But with quiet confidence that the Lord directs your steps (Proverbs 16:9).

A Life of Peaceful, Purposeful Choices

Balanced decision-making won't always make life easier, but it will make it holier.

It invites you to:

- Respond instead of react.

- Reflect instead of rush.

- Discern instead of default.

- It's not flashy. It's not always fast. But it's faithful.

And that's the kind of life we're called to live, rooted in truth, led by the Spirit, seasoned with wisdom, and saturated in love.

Let's Walk This Road Together

Keep growing. Keep praying. Keep helping others walk wisely. Remember, God is still writing in your heart whenever you approach Him. And He writes in your heart His wisdom, grace, and glory.

Your Next Steps:

Reflect on one decision you're currently facing. Walk it through the principles you've learned. Use the Decision Work Sheet found at the end of the book. Refer to the index of scriptures on areas requiring a decision.

Share this journey with someone else. Invite them to walk with you.

Revisit this book when needed. Let it be a tool, not a trophy.

And when you're unsure, return to this simple prayer:

"Lord, help me hear Your voice above all others. Calm my emotions, sharpen my mind, and lead me in Your perfect peace. I trust You more than I trust myself. Amen."

◆ ◆ § ◆ ◆

As we come to the end, I pray you will grow in your ability to make Godly decisions you won't regret.

I leave you with two final thoughts. Why two? Because they are really complementary and speak to the importance of the underlying principles and the consequences of your decisions.

"It's not hard to make decisions when you know what your values are."
~Roy E. Disney

"I am not a product of my circumstances. I am a product of my decisions."
~ Stephen Covey

Appendix

Practical tools, scriptural depth, and decision-making clarity ... right when you need it most.

How to Use This Appendix

This section isn't just an add-on; it's a companion for the road ahead. Whether you're facing a major life choice or wrestling with day-to-day decisions, the tools here are designed to ground you in wisdom, sharpen your focus, and tune your ear to God's leading.

Use this appendix when:

- You're overwhelmed and unsure what to do next.

- You feel paralyzed by emotion or pressure.

- You want to teach others how to make godly decisions.

- You need a reset in your thinking, praying, or planning.

Included in this section:

- A printable Decision-Making Worksheet

- A curated Scripture **Index** organized by theme

This page left blank intentionally.

Decision-Making Worksheet

Use this worksheet as a journal prompt or group study tool.
Print and revisit it as often as needed.

Step One: Clarify the Decision

What is the decision I'm facing?
(Be specific and concise)

Step Two: Identify Your Emotions

What emotions am I feeling about this decision?
(Check all that apply)

☐ Fear

☐ Anxiety

☐ Excitement

☐ Guilt

☐ Hope

☐ Anger

☐ Sadness

☐ Peace

☐ Confusion

☐ Other: _____

What might be fueling these emotions?

_____

Step Three: Seek God's Voice

What Scriptures come to mind? *(Use the index below for help.)*

- What is God's character in this area?

  _____

- What biblical principles apply here?

  _____

Step 4: Gather the Facts

What do I know?

- Objective truth

  _____

- Specific scriptures providing instruction

  _____

- Established Biblical principles providing guidance

  _____

- What do I assume (speculation or fear)?

  _____

- What do I need to **research** or confirm?

  _____

Step 5: Pray Intentionally

☐ Have I asked God for wisdom? (James 1:5)

☐ Am I willing to obey, even if it's hard or uncomfortable?

☐ Am I rushing out of emotion or waiting on God's timing?

Step 6: Seek Counsel

- Who are the wise, Spirit-filled people I can ask for input?

  _____

- What feedback or caution have I already received?

  _____

Step 7: Decide with Peace

- What is the next faithful step I can take today?

  _____

- Am I experiencing God's peace, even if it doesn't feel easy? _____

- What step requires faith, not fear, to move forward?

  _____

This page left blank intentionally.

Scripture Index (By Theme)

Quick-reference guide for real-time spiritual guidance

Wisdom & Discernment

Proverbs 3:5–6 – Trust in the Lord with all your heart

James 1:5 – Ask God for wisdom, and He will give it

Proverbs 18:15 – A discerning heart seeks knowledge

Colossians 1:9 – Pray to be filled with spiritual wisdom

Emotions & Self-Control

Proverbs 25:28 – A person without self-control is defenseless

Galatians 5:22–23 – Fruit of the Spirit includes self-control

Psalm 42:5 – Speak truth to your soul when you're downcast

2 Corinthians 10:5 – Take every thought captive to Christ

Fear & Trust

Isaiah 41:10 – Do not fear, God is with you

Philippians 4:6–7 – Don't be anxious; bring it to God

2 Timothy 1:7 – God gave us power, love, and a sound mind

Romans 8:31 – If God is for us, who can be against us?

God's Guidance

Psalm 32:8 – "I will instruct you and teach you..."

John 16:13 – The Spirit of truth will guide you

Proverbs 16:9 – We plan, but God directs

Psalm 119:105 – God's Word is a lamp to our feet

Peace & Patience

Isaiah 26:3 – God keeps in perfect peace those who trust Him

Psalm 46:10 – Be still and know that He is God

Galatians 6:9 – Don't grow weary in doing good

Ecclesiastes 3:1 – There is a time for every purpose under heaven

Relational Decisions

Romans 12:18 – As far as it depends on you, live in peace

Ephesians 4:15 – Speak the truth in love

Proverbs 13:20 – Walk with the wise, become wise

Matthew 18:15 – Go directly to someone when resolving a conflict

Forgiveness & Restoration

Matthew 6:12 – Forgive as we are forgiven

Colossians 3:13 – Bear with each other and forgive

2 Corinthians 5:17–18 – Ministry of reconciliation

Luke 6:37 – Don't judge or condemn; forgive

Calling & Purpose

Ephesians 2:10 – Created for good works prepared by God

Romans 12:1–2 – Offer yourself, be transformed

1 Peter 4:10 – Use your gifts to serve others

Proverbs 19:21 – Many plans, but God's purpose prevails

References And Further Reading

[1]Damasio, Antonio R. Descartes' Error: Emotion, Reason, and the Human Brain. New York: Grosset/Putnam, 1994. https://books.google.com/books?id=eeOZAAAAIAAJ

◆ ◆ § ◆ ◆

If you lliked this book, please leave a review. Thanks – James B. Fannin

Other Books and eBooks Available Online by James B. Fannin

Is It Ever Too Late to Start Saving for Retirement?: Concerned You Might Have Waited Too Long?

Passive Income for Life or Retirement: What it is, Why you need it, Ways you can get it

What Are You Thinking?: How to Get In Tune with God

Encouragement - Not Just a Suggestion

The Golden Rule 2.0: A New Path for a Time Such as This

Fun and Challenging Word Search Puzzles for Adults: Solutions Included - Suitable for All Adults

✨ Light for the Road Ahead

> *"For this reason we also, since the day we heard about it, have not ceased praying for you and asking that you may be filled with the knowledge of His will in all spiritual wisdom and understanding."*
> *— Colossians 1:9 (NASB)*

May these words guide you as you step into each decision with faith. May your choices be shaped by His wisdom, steadied by His truth, and guided by His light on the road ahead.

~ Sincerely,
James B. Fannin

Notes

_____

_____

_____

_____

_____

_____

_____

_____

_____

_____

_____

Decision Questions

What is the most difficult decision you have ever made? _____

_____

Why was it hard? _____

_____

What decision are you currently putting off, or will soon have to make? _____

_____

Have you tried using the Decision-Making Worksheet? _____ Did it help? _____

I am always looking for feedback on ways it could be improved, and/or on the success you have had using it. Please send your feedback here:
narrowchoice@jamesbfannin.com

Page Left Blank Intentionally

www.ingramcontent.com/pod-product-compliance
Lightning Source LLC
Chambersburg PA
CBHW071633140626
46555CB00022B/2701